PLACES ALONG THE WAY

PLACES ALONG THE WAY

Meditations on the Journey of Faith

Martin Marty and Micah Marty

Augsburg
MINNEAPOLIS

PLACES ALONG THE WAY
Meditations on the Journey of Faith

Photographs copyright © Micah Marty. Portions of the text were first published in *Places Along the Way: A Lenten Pilgrimage* by Martin E. Marty, copyright © 1992 Augsburg Fortress.

Scripture quotations are from New Revised Standard Version Bible, copyright 1989 Division of Christian Education of the National Council of the Churches of Christ in the United States of America. Used by permission.

Prayer marked *LBW* is from *Lutheran Book of Worship*, copyright © 1978.

Cover design: Koechel Peterson & Associates, Inc.
Interior design: Micah Marty
Separations and film assembly: Professional Litho, Inc.

Library of Congress Cataloging-in-Publication Data

Marty, Martin E., 1928-
    Places along the way : meditations on the journey of faith /
Martin Marty, Micah Marty.
      p.   cm.
    Includes bibliographical references.
    ISBN 0-8066-2746-8
    1. Lent—Prayer-books and devotions—English. 2. Devotional
calendars. 3. Palestine—Pictorial works. 4. Christian pilgrims
and pilgrimages—Palestine—Prayer-books and devotions—English.
I. Marty, Micah, 1960- . II. Title.
BV85.M364 1994
242'.34—dc20   94-29532
                                                     CIP

Manufactured in the U.S.A.   AF 9-2746
                                         7   8   9   10

Author's Introduction

For the next forty-seven days you and I are going to be on a figurative journey together. "You" are any one of thousands who I hope will be fellow pilgrims visiting the "places along the way" in this book. "I" will introduce myself in a moment. Together we make up some of the "we" who appear within these pages. That "we" includes all on the journey, all pilgrims, all believers, for we are a common company.

That company is called by the name of Christ, in whose name we begin each day and in whose name you may end the prayers printed in this book. To undertake a spiritual journey in Christ's name is different from just being "spiritual" in the fashion of our day. Spirituality is often seen as something one possesses or aspires to or brags about having. It is often the language of people who say that somehow they are God or God is in them. They undertake disciplines to deepen the resources of their soul. They are serious and often admirable. We are companions of theirs on the general human venture and share membership in the human family.

For this spiritual journey, however, we begin with the knowledge that we are distant from God, who often seems absent from our scene. We know that we are in need and that God has to help us, re-create us, and then guide us. We do not make up the plot of our own spiritual journey. The Bible provides the plot for our own "pilgrim's progress" and refers to the landmark places along the way.

The "I" who joins you on this journey is author and partner with the photographer. The most important thing for you to know about me is that this wayfarer, like his companions, is someone who lives with faith and doubt, joys and disappointments, setbacks and hopes. Less important, but helpful: I am an historian who tells the story of the wandering people of God in our own centuries, an editor who chronicles their daily doings, a family person who hopes that generations to come will share the journey, a writer who loves to author books like this, a pastor who for a third of a century has not had a specific flock but who relates generally to those of others anywhere. I hope that the voice of the Scriptures comes through in these pages about contemporary life and that as you share this book with others, our company will continue to grow in numbers and experience growth in grace.

Martin E. Marty

Photographer's Introduction

Places matter to us as individuals, whether they are places we inhabit or visit, frequent or remember. Through our life experiences we come to see them as more than physical locations, often associating them with people, events, and ideas. As a photographer of landscapes and cityscapes, I believe strongly in the importance of *place* in our lives, both private places (home places) and public places (communal places).

This book is designed to combine these two, the public and the private, in the same way that a church does. There, as here, we are "together" in the same place, benefiting from each other and yet each bringing our own unique past and direction. Through the photographs, I am providing a common meeting place to be shared by those of us who produced this book and those of you who use it to make your own spiritual journey. We meet at the photographs, but we each see the places through our own eyes.

The photographs are intended to provide a clearer image of each place while leaving plenty of room for your unique reflection and interpretation. They are to offer help as you form your own mental pictures of the places described on the pages. And for those (like me!) who have trouble concentrating on some spiritual meditations without their mind drifting, the photographs provide a specific daily focus, tying each reflection to a distinctive place.

I come to this project as a photographer who is often uncomfortable sharing his work. Most of the pictures I make are primarily intended to meet my own needs, and the privacy I feel about my purpose in a typical photograph is probably exceeded only by the privacy I feel about my own spiritual journey (far from over as it is). But illustrating these "places along the way" presented an irresistible challenge and an appealing opportunity. It presented the challenge of combining my photographs with words (both new and old) that could multiply their impact, and it offered the opportunity to work with an author who shares my aesthetic perspective on places (or more accurately, I inherited *his* aesthetic!).

The photographer Edward Weston once said, "When I hear Bach in my pictures, I know I've succeeded." While I have no such lofty aspirations, I hope that you find harmony in these words and pictures—and that the book will inspire you to wake up each morning to the prospect of a new dawn in your faith.

Micah Marty

Brief notes on the photographs can be found on pages 106–109.

One Day, One Page,
One Place, One Prayer

Advice to someone on any journey: take it one day at a time. And observe the places along the way.

Advice to someone on a spiritual journey: take this book one page at a time. And again, observe the pictured places along the way.

On a pilgrimage through a physical landscape, the pilgrim is content with a view of the current surroundings, leaving tomorrow's sights for tomorrow.

On a spiritual pilgrimage through this pictured landscape, it is best to encounter the sites one page at a time.

A prescription for the traveler with us, for the good of your soul: turn a page each morning, read the suggested scripture, study the picture, say the prayer. Keep these in mind through the day, for use in times of study or times of doubt, when you need encouragement or would be delighted. These reflections can help during times of temptation, hours of boredom, moments of uncertainty; between appointments, at the desk, before a nap. Then at the end of the day, upon retiring, return to the book, the reading, the picture.

For such purposes, keep the book open, as we do at our house: on a book stand, music stand, bedside table, or desk top.

Let the photographs (and the photographer's notes on pages 106–109) evoke for you the biblical moments encountered on this journey. The depictions of biblical scenes are not literal historical references to archaeological sites. The streams, caves, mountains, cities, and clouds pictured here are instead intended to stimulate the imagination of those who would grow in grace and deepen their spirituality.

Some of you will want to take this book-related journey during Lent; if you start on Ash Wednesday, you will finish on Easter. (To help you keep your place during that time, Sundays are marked with an asterisk in the "Notes on the Photographs" section beginning on page 106.) But start over immediately after Lent, or begin the figurative trip any day, and you will find that during the next forty-seven days these scriptures will reach the soul, as, we hope, the photographs and readings will.

Chaos

Genesis 1:1-5
The earth was a formless void.

Chaos is the name of a place in Greek myth. In the second verse of the Bible it is the name of a condition, *tohuvebohu*, a Hebrew word that has not survived as clearly as the Greek but that evokes similar responses. *Chaos* has become the word for the way we naturally regard life around us, as we face a new day, a new season. How can we overcome chaos? How can we think of it at all?

A formless void: so it was to the writer of Genesis. Chaos was what God had to work with when dividing light from darkness, day from night.

A formless void: God still has to work with it. The news headlines and television reports come at us with sometimes blinding, sometimes darkening descriptions of chaos. How, ask the mind and soul, will I get through the day in a world described by such news items?

A formless void: God works with *tohuvebohu*, or chaos, in our personal lives. In the back of the mind, leftover guilt may do its haunting. In the front of the mind are worries that will not let us be free. God in Christ then addresses our chaos. The pathway in the days ahead will take us to the cross where perfect love reorders our world. God, being generous, has our cares and needs in mind.

Lead us, Creator, out of chaos
through a day ordered by your love,
as it is your will to do. Amen

Eden

Genesis 3:22-24
*The Lord God sent the man forth from the garden of Eden,
to till the ground from which he was taken.*

Eden, the garden of God, is a place that we will not find on literal maps, the first such place on our journey. Eden now is like a dream, a result of imagination, something evoked by memory. Paradise, we may call it: the perfect situation for humans to enjoy each other, their world, their God. If only . . .

If only we could go back to paradise, all would be well. So we think. But each day we see evidence that we do not naturally belong under the gaze of God.

If only we could go ahead to the coming paradise, a new Eden. But we cannot escape into the future. We walk our paths in a world that, in a way, remembers one Eden and looks forward to another.

If only we could recognize the value of the days after and before paradise. The creator chooses to let us till the ground. The farmers among us know what that means. The rest of us, denied Eden, get to find our own meaning in each day.

After Eden we get to live lives of work, of challenge in pain and loss, of delight in health and gain, of service in the face of human need, of gratitude for the Christ.

*Denied the perfection of an Eden, we live, O Lord,
ready for the tasks and gifts you give us. Amen*

Nod

Genesis 4:1-16
*Then Cain went away from the presence of the Lord,
and settled in the land of Nod, east of Eden.*

Nod, east of Eden. A place no one could locate, even in the time of biblical writings. It is therefore reasonable to ask, what do people at the end of the twentieth century have to do with an ancient place we cannot locate on a map? How are we to imagine it? A barren landscape? A city? A place for meandering in bewilderment and shame?

According to Genesis, after farmer Cain killed his shepherd brother, Abel, the Lord drove Cain away from the soil. God would henceforth be hidden from his face. Cain, in fear, went into exile in Nod, which evidently meant in Hebrew a "homeless" or "aimless" place.

There may be times when we feel settled, "in place." This is especially the case if things are going well in the home, family, workplace, and circles of friendship. But we, too, are wanderers, roaming east of Eden, in Nod. We sometimes may feel driven away because of something we have done or may experience the hiddenness of God. We can be on the run from our past, fearful for the future, ill at ease in the present.

We wander thus. We wander, that is, until God reassures us: "Though you are not yet home and your exile is not ended, I am with you." With that promise, our wanderings find direction and purpose.

*Hide not your face from us, O Lord, but guide our wanderings
and give meaning to our pilgrimage. Amen*

Ararat

Genesis 8:4; 9:8-17
The ark came to rest on the mountains of Ararat.
There God said, "I am establishing my covenant with you."

Ararat. Our journey, which began as a walk, has quickly become a climb. At a high place called Ararat, according to the Genesis account, a survivor named Noah went out, with his family, from the ark where God had helped them outlast a great global flood. "God remembered Noah" (8:1).

A universal flood, a crowded ark, a mountaintop landing, and a divine rescue are so far from our experience that they seem irrelevant. Why stop at this point on our pilgrimage?

We stop for good reason: to remind ourselves that God remembers us, cooped up wherever we are, worthy of no favor, yet memorable recipients of divine care.

The story climaxes when God provides a rainbow as a sign. The rainbow is a reminder to God: "I will see it and remember the everlasting covenant between God and every living creature."

It is really we, however, who need the reminding. We may not find necessary the sight of an actual mountain or rainbow. Entirely through our ears when they are reached by the word of God, and through hearts touched by that word, comes our awareness that the creator re-creates, the giver of life keeps giving.

Remember your covenant, as you promised,
O Creator and Re-creator, for in it we are secure. Amen

Babel

It was called Babel, because there the Lord
confused the language of all the earth.

Babel. This towered stop is one of the most confusing to the spiritual seeker. But confusion was planned into the plot: here the Lord "confused the language." Ever after, humans must ask, how will we now find our way?

Every thoughtful traveler asks directions before going toward any strange place. When lost, most of us ask our way, especially if there are no maps. Yet how can we make sense of the answer if the answerer speaks a language we do not know? To be in a strange and unfamiliar place can be menacing. Locals may scowl or laugh when we speak in ways incomprehensible to them. They may threaten, but in a language we cannot understand. They may be generous and offer something good, but we fail to catch the point.

Confusion of languages, according to the Babel story, resulted from an act of human pride, a desire by people, as they said in Genesis, "to make a name for ourselves." But God scattered them, intending that they experience confusion and, in their dispersal, cease pursuing their destructive ways.

God's final word, however, is not that there be human confusion. In all languages, God speaks a reconciling word. Among all peoples the humbled can be brought together. The creator, now in Christ, reconciles people and peoples and brings the scattered together. On this pilgrimage, amid crowded and confusing signs, we remain well aware that we live among the dispersed and bewildered. But God, the gatherer, never wants to let us remain lost. Amid the confusion of tongues, the divine promise speaks clearly.

God of grace, even as we are confused by claims and counterclaims,
hostile voices and alien tongues,
let us hear your clear word: be reconciled. Amen

Ur

Genesis 11:31–12:3
They went out together from Ur. The Lord said to Abram,
"Go from your country to the land that I will show you."

Ur: On the map of our journey, this is the shortest name. But it stands for one of the longest adventures, one that still continues. From Ur of the Chaldeans, Abram (later Abraham) was called by God. The story continues: Abram responded.

The New Testament makes sense of this: "By faith Abraham obeyed when he was called to set out for a place . . . and he set out, not knowing where he was going." He continued because "he looked forward to the city that has foundations, whose architect and builder is God" (Hebrews 11:8,10).

Suddenly the old stories from Genesis start sounding like part of our own autobiographies. We are children of Abraham and Sarah, children of promise. They are ancestors of Jesus, who daily makes the promise ever more clear.

We go out today and tomorrow not knowing where the steps will take us. We will be tempted to become attached to the wrong places and things. We are likely to put our minds on cities without foundations, built by humans who are destined to be dust. But the Christ of promise gives us the vision and confidence to walk in faith, with eyes fixed on the permanent.

Architect and builder of the human places where we spend our lives,
keep our vision focused on the eternal foundations. Amen

Shechem

Genesis 12:4-7
Abram passed through the land to the place at Shechem.
He built there an altar to the Lord, who had appeared to him.

Shechem. Abram's stopping place, and ours this day, is the first Palestinian site named in the Bible. Here the migrating Abram camped at the oak of Moreh, surrounded by Canaanites who did not know the Lord. And here the Lord appeared to Abram, promising to give this place to him and his offspring.

The book of Genesis, it has been said, is less a story of how the world began than of how God's people became God's people. The Old Testament helps us see ourselves as children of Abraham, members of a people to whom God appeared.

Like Abram, we are surrounded by signs that the world does not know the Lord: war, greed, hatred, poverty. God seems to have vanished from so much of our scene, and we are distressed or seduced in our own strange places.

God's vanishing is only an appearance and not the last word about where we spend this day. Now, as in Abram's day, God appears in the midst of and over against the altars of those who do not know God. Yet often we try to distract ourselves from focusing on the truly divine. Shechem is the pilgrimage stop that tells us that any place is the place for the Lord to appear. Any time is the time for the sacred Word to reach us with guidance and promise.

In all your surprising ways, but chiefly through your Word, O Lord, appear to us, address us, offer us the hope you promise. Amen

Mamre

Genesis 18:1-15
The Lord appeared to Abraham by the oaks of Mamre.
Abraham looked up and saw three men standing near him.

Mamre. At so many places on our pilgrimage we read stories of how God appeared, stories that prefigure God's appearances now in our day.

This time, near another altar Abraham built and in front of a tent where the migrant lived, God visited Abraham. The appearance was in the form of three angels. The plot of the story is a bit obscure, but the message is not: "You, old man, and your wife Sarah, the barren one, are to have a child and countless descendants."

Sarah laughed—good for her!—because she was a person of common sense, ordinary observation, and wisdom about her body. But "by faith [Abraham] received power of procreation . . . because he considered him faithful who had promised" (Hebrews 11:11). And Sarah's skeptical laughter turned to the joyful cry of the mother-to-be.

We are a long way from Mamre with its oaks and tents, from Sarah's bread making and Abraham's offer of water with which to wash feet. Under our oaks, no angelic visitors come, no visible strangers enter our tents to wash, rest, share bread—or to speak for God, as God.

Or do they? Listen to the word of promise. Is the message for us? God's creative activity continues to this day.

Let us, by bringing in the stranger, know that we entertain angels unaware. And let those who bring the Word speak your promise, God of truth. Amen

Moriah

Genesis 22:1-19
God said, "Take your only son Isaac, whom you love, and
go to the land of Moriah, and offer him there as a burnt offering."

Moriah. We admit to ourselves that this is a stop we would rather avoid on our journey. The story of what happened here, what almost happened here, is one of the most jarring and distasteful in the Bible. Abraham was to take a knife to his son's heart, kill him, and burn him—as an offering to God.

Let that kind of thing happen today and we would imprison and shun Abraham for life. That the story has a happy ending does not detract from the horror it breeds. It does not diminish the terror in imagining what Isaac must have felt as he looked up from the altar. Avoid Moriah.

Despite the abhorrent details, this grimly fascinating story does serve as a landmark for us who hear no voices, who in humaneness would shun such a call. Genesis tells the story as an example of a supreme test, which Abraham met in faith. Confident that God would not break the promises, knowing that Isaac was the only hope for Abraham's line to continue, Abraham obeyed.

We do not have to hear voices or seek tests of faith beyond those that come in the ordinary course of daily temptations and adventures. Even on the smaller scales of our own lives, we find the calls of God dramatic, the promises fulfilled.

Give us strength, Lord of hope, according to your pleasure,
to meet the tests of faith and to hear your voice
in the quiet summonings of this day. Amen

Bethel

Genesis 28:10-22
*Jacob called that place Bethel. There he said, "This stone, which I have
set up for a pillar, shall be God's house."*

Bethel. Here we are, we moderns, still following an ancient family: the family of
Abraham and Sarah and son Isaac, of Isaac and Rebekah and son Jacob. We see
our story in their story and find our place amid their places.

So today *Bethel*—"the house of God"—is the name we still give to
places where we hope to encounter God in the divine Word, prayer, the washing of baptism, the receiving of the bread and wine at the Lord's Table.

The first Bethel was the site of a famous dream in which Jacob, while
on a journey, saw a ladder full of angels and heard a voice: "I am the Lord, the
God of Abraham your father and the God of Isaac. . . . Know that I am with
you and will keep you wherever you go."

We know that God keeps us also now. Yet often in our Bethels and our
own houses we neglect the signs. So too, for a time, did Jacob: "Surely the Lord
is in this place—and I did not know it!"

Jacob soon "knew it." He gave us the example and then the vision to
know the Lord in the places of our walks and rest.

*When you come to us in your house and our house, Lord, help us recognize
your presence and welcome your being with us. Amen*

Peniel

Genesis 32:22-32
Jacob called the place Peniel, saying,
"For I have seen God face to face, and yet my life is preserved."

Peniel. It means "the face of God" and is a site we visit, though we have not seen the face of God. No one can see God's face and live, said God to Moses. Yet we identify with Jacob, who named this place along the river Jabbok "Peniel" after wrestling there at night with "a man."

This story is mysterious: Was the "man" God? An angel? An unidentifiable sacred figure? Jacob's other side—"bad Jacob" wrestling with "good Jacob"? Whoever the "man" was, Jacob saw in his wrestling and in the blessing that followed it "the face of God."

Sufferers through the ages have sympathized with Jacob in this scene. Those who have wrestled with addictions, chronic disease, a spiritual affliction, an awareness of their limits, know they will never get over the "limp" they carry after the encounter.

The same people—any and all of us—also can hear their voice in Jacob's: "I will not let you go, unless you bless me." The wound and the blessing: these come always together. And often the blessing is more vivid.

We will not let you go, God of mystery, unless you bless us.
Let us see you in our wrestlings and wounds. Amen

Goshen

Genesis 46:28–47:6
*The land of Egypt is before you; settle your father and your brothers
in the best part of the land; let them live in the land of Goshen.*

Goshen. This is a place for the promise of hospitality. The children of Israel, with whom we identify, were strangers; in the Genesis account they even called themselves aliens. Yet Pharaoh let these refugee shepherds live in "the land of Goshen," which was "the best part of the land."

You will not find Goshen today. Some think it was at Wadi Tumilat, but their guess is no better than ours. So we imagine "the best part of the land" to be anywhere on the flat but not featureless Delta, where there are streamlets and canals. Picture scene one with an abundance of flowing water for the flocks.

Scene two: in the course of time Israel will be enslaved and Pharaoh's promises to them forgotten. The waters will no longer freely flow and the people will not be free to move about. They will know disappointment, as hospitality turns sour.

Goshen is still here for us: a signal of hospitality, a place of refuge in beautiful surroundings. But we do well not to get attached to any place connected with human promise. Those who give us a place can take it away; those who open a door can close it. We are to enjoy our surroundings without thinking of them as lasting. "The best part of the land" can know disaster. God, not Pharaoh, is the promise keeper who provides us with a good place to be. We find refuge in the divine protection, where the streams never cease to flow and where no one can take us captive. We walk today in that sense of freedom, experiencing freshness while tending, in most cases, not flocks but to daily tasks, finding liberty in the path we get to walk.

*Generous God, in our lands today as in Goshen of old,
let your people find hospitality—and return it, with generous hearts. Amen*

The Nile

Exodus 2:1-10
The daughter of Pharaoh named the child Moses,
"because," she said, "I drew him out of the water."

The Nile. The Nile is mighty, but this Exodus story is about weakness. The story's lead character is Moses, who became mighty as Israel's lawgiver and leader, but here is as helpless as an abandoned child. The daughter of Pharaoh, bathing, hears a cry and finds the baby in a basket. Moses is turned over to his own mother, who fulfills her role as his nursemaid and nurturer.

Like so many important stories about powerful people, this one is full of near-misses, frailties, and flaws. Moses was almost lost and remained dependent upon his mother, his watchful sister Miriam, and the bathing princess, until in adulthood he was shocked and pressed into serving the enslaved people of Israel.

Fix in your mind the baby Moses as a reminder that we—on our own journeys—are not self-reliant, all-powerful pathfinders and makers of our way. We are under the careful eye of God.

Notice us, watchful God, in our weakness and abandonment,
and grace us with alert eyes and loving hands to care for others. Amen

Horeb

Exodus 3:1-12
At Horeb, the mountain of God, the angel of the Lord
appeared to Moses in a flame of fire out of a bush.

Horeb. The mountain of God. Here Moses was stunned and stirred in a scene that inspires us as well. He saw a bush that kept burning and heard a voice.

The voice commanded Moses not to come closer but to remove his sandals ("for the place on which you are standing is holy ground"). Soon the barefoot Israelite learned that God had heard the cries of suffering Israel and that he was to lead the people out of Egypt.

This story leads us to ask, are we ever capable of experiencing the holy?

We need no fiery shrubs, no voice from the bushes. Our chapels, cathedrals, closets, offices, and kitchens serve as places for us to humble ourselves. Then, in prayer, while hearing the Word or recognizing the presence of Christ, we have occasion to show awe, as did Moses. Then we are ready to hear God's call to respond in our day. And we shall so respond.

Fire us with visions of what you would have us do, God of Israel.
Whisper a call and grant us the gift of response, and we shall follow. Amen

The Red Sea

Exodus 13:18; 14:15-31
*God led the people toward the Red Sea and turned the sea
into dry land. Thus the Lord saved Israel.*

The Red Sea, better translated "the Sea of Reeds," created a natural barrier that threatened to prevent Israel's escape from Egypt and the encroaching army of enslavers.

"By a strong east wind all night"—that sounds natural enough—the Lord dried this Sea of Reeds. After Israel had passed through, "the waters returned and covered . . . the entire army of Pharaoh." That sounds more than natural. Clearly we are being asked to see God's guiding hand in wind and sea.

We do. In a service of Baptism we are reminded that God led Israel by the pillar of cloud and fire through the sea. Now we are delivered from whatever forms an obstacle between us and the freedom of God in Christ.

Would this deliverance mean more to us if it came with special effects from Hollywood? Not necessarily. Many in Israel soon forgot the guiding hand. They rebelled or murmured, forgetting the wind and the drying of a sea.

Miracles can occur without special effects. It takes more doing for a holy God to forgive an errant person than it does to part the waters of a sea. And God does that forgiving, delivering here and now. The clean heart and right spirit result.

*O Lord, as you delivered Israel, deliver us; as you guided the people,
guide each and all of us; as you cared for them, care now for us. Amen*

40

The Sinai Desert

Exodus 19:1-6
They came into the wilderness of Sinai, and the Lord God said,
"I bore you on eagles' wings and brought you to myself."

Sinai. When we think of it, we usually think of the mountain where God met Moses in the burning bush and later gave the Ten Commandments. But Sinai is also a wilderness, a desert place where Israel assembled and God spoke. God still speaks.

When God speaks, it is often to remind Israel and us of what has already happened. But just as often the word of God deals with the future. At Sinai the people received the covenant: God would be their God and they would be God's people.

Why rely on such a covenant? Here is where remembering what has happened is the issue. "You have seen what I did to the Egyptians, and how I bore you on eagles' wings." If the people would keep the covenant, God said, they would be God's "treasured possession out of all the peoples."

That covenant and that promise can easily be distorted and perverted. The "we" who have the privilege of identifying with Israel and reading ourselves into their situation can turn forgetful (there goes the covenant!) or prideful (there goes God!). We then claim that we had all the achievements.

God, however, offers us a greater security by reminding us how helpless we would be in the wilderness of life, in the desert places of the spirit. Look up and imagine eagles soaring. On their backs are eaglets, Israel's representatives and ours. We need only cling to the one who soars, who rescues. Being a "treasured possession" is a gift, not an achievement. It is, therefore, secure.

We would know the exhilaration of soaring,
the freedom that comes with rescue, the security of being your possession,
and pray that these be ours today, thanks to your care. Amen

Nebo

Deuteronomy 32:48–33:1, 28-29
God said to Moses, "Ascend Mount Nebo; you shall die there."
And Moses blessed the Israelites, saying,
"Happy are you, O Israel, a people saved by the Lord."

Nebo is one name for the high place from which Moses was allowed to see the land of promise. He could look through the morning mists across the ranges and glimpse, in the distance, the countryside to which Israel had been called. Yet he was not allowed to enter that land.

It is natural to question God's harsh choice to frustrate Moses' dream. The two incidents that prompted God to say, "[Moses] broke faith with me among the Israelites," would strike most people as having been minor disobediences. Moses, a leader of Israel for decades, had good cause to sulk. He might even have been led to complaint or rage by the curt word, "Although you may view the land from a distance, you shall not enter it." But instead we read one line later, "Moses, the man of God, blessed the Israelites before his death."

In Moses' song of blessing in Deuteronomy 33, there is no hint of anything except the sound of exulting in the joy of Israel. Moses foresees Israel living "in safety, untroubled . . . in a land of grain and wine."

Something of the spirit of Moses in this story marks true leaders or people of integrity in any role. The great ones fulfill their duties, aware of their limits and faults. They are then able to enjoy the results of their good labors, even when these results work mainly to the benefit of others. We build for the generations that follow. God authorizes the blessing, and we are blessed.

Happy are we when we walk in the path of Israel,
as it responded to your good call
and welcomed your good care, Lord God. Amen

Persia

Isaiah 44:24–45:7
***The Lord says of Cyrus, "He is my shepherd,
and he shall carry out all my purpose."***

Persia is unnamed in today's text, but we recognize the place because we know that Cyrus was the first to rule there. Cyrus did what kings do: he built towered fortresses and strong walls from which his armies marched to conquer. He called himself king of the world, great king, legitimate king.

The God he did not recognize or even know had other names for him, however: "my shepherd" and the "anointed" of the Lord. From that naming we learn much about how God governs our human affairs.

When Persia became the challenger to Babylon, Cyrus came to be the agent of rescue for exiled Israel. He was the human who made their return from Babylon possible. He was the divine instrument.

God named Cyrus, though Cyrus could not name God. This is astonishing. Cyrus worked the purpose of God, though he did not know God. Maybe we should not readily dismiss secular leaders as being merely secular or think of governments as being godless. They can serve the purposes of God.

Where do people fit who do not not know God, who do not believe in the Lord, and yet serve divine intentions? Today we will be open to seeing the care of God through all sorts of people. And we will see such people differently. We may even associate rulers not merely with towers and fortresses and armies but with liberating policies, as God guides them.

Our souls are not satisfied by the actions of those who do not know God, nor have these people come to saving health. But their works of government and justice, of leadership and care, serve the purposes of God.

*Help us recognize your work, O Lord, in the acts of those who, not yet knowing
you, do your works of justice in the world. Amen*

Babylon

Jeremiah 29:1-14
Seek the welfare of Babylon, where I have sent you into exile,
for in its welfare you will find your welfare.

Babylon. A place of exile. Conquerors lead victims on paths to exile. Liberators release captives on paths to freedom. During exile, these captives have a choice of paths. They may choose to follow none or to dream of roads to different places. Or they may choose to follow paths that beckon with opportunity. Today we associate this choice of ways with Babylon.

The ancient people of God were in exile in Babylon, but God did not abandon them there. In the text for today we get to read someone else's mail. Jeremiah sent the exiles a letter from Jerusalem. That letter comes to us as well.

Home to each of us is our house or apartment, our living room, nursing home room, dormitory room; it is the favorite chair, the place where the spoons are kept, the neighborhood, the local church.

We are not wholly at home in or with any of them, however. Part of the heart and mind feels exiled. With Adam, Eve, and all sinners, we have been driven from Eden. With Abraham we seek the eternal city and have not found it. With the first followers of Jesus we sometimes feel distant from the beloved Christ. With Augustine our hearts are restless and will find no repose until they rest in the one who made us. The world around us belongs to powers not under our control. Everything seems temporary, passing. Not much seems worth doing. If only we could follow the paths away from where we are called to be.

Then we open this mail and learn that no matter where we are, even in Babylon, we are to build, live, plant, eat, have families, pray for our city and its surroundings, and seek its welfare. And when we do, God, as announced in Jeremiah and in the gospel of Christ, provides "a future with hope."

We search for you with all our heart, God of the ages.
Let us find you and be brought back to have a future with you. Amen

Chebar

Ezekiel 1:1-3; 33:11-16
*By the river Chebar the word of the Lord came to the priest Ezekiel,
and the hand of the Lord was on him there.*

Chebar. A watercourse, a canal in Babylon, was an unlikely place for a prophet of God to receive a vision. On first thought, Chebar seems to be even less relevant to our day than the Babylon or Persia of yesterday and yesteryears.

On second thought, however, thanks to the revelations that came to Isaiah, Jeremiah, and Ezekiel and to the scriptures that came from their hands, those distant places live in our imagination. Now, what about the bizarre vision received along this stream named Chebar?

Ezekiel, the priest in exile, lived with exiles. He seems to have been the wild-man visionary. His unsettling dreams often give some interpreters today the impulse to misapply his figurative words to our literal world.

Ezekiel, stunned—the stunning lasted seven days!—by his call, also had insight into the kind of world in which we live. A great denouncer of God's errant people, he brings a most serious note to us in the wayward parts of our journey, our strayings from the straight path of pilgrimage.

In the midst of the eccentricities and strangeness of Ezekiel, however, come words that to the Christian ear speak sweetly: God takes no pleasure in the death of the wicked. God wills that we turn and that, by grace we can hear, we "shall surely live."

Stun us by the power of the ancient prophecies that still speak;
stir us by their eloquence; shake us with your judgment;
save us with grace, merciful God. Amen

Sheol

Hosea 13:14; 14:1-9
Shall I ransom them from the power of Sheol?
Shall I redeem them from Death?
I will love them freely.

Sheol. This is the shadowland, the depths with no exit, the utterly depressing place. It represents the threat to our continuing pilgrimage and marks its limits. Sheol was the netherworld, the dark underground, the world's pit. Dead and departed spirits were supposed to dwell there. Who praised God in Sheol?

Hosea, the weeping prophet who spoke of Sheol, knew something about disappointment and despair over human existence. His book seems to be a parable based on his own marriage to a faithless prostitute. This parable depicts God's frequently frustrated goal of being faithful to faithless Israel. The response of Hosea was to pronounce judgment, judgment, judgment.

We could not endure the image of Sheol in Hosea's words were it not for the last chapter of his prophecy. There he answers yes to God's questions about rescue from Sheol. Yes, God shall ransom people. Yes, God shall redeem them from death and offer life.

Repentant Israel and we, turning and returning to the God we know in Christ, hear the promise: "I will heal their disloyalty; I will love them freely." Hosea adds a note: "Those who are wise understand these things." The ways of the Lord are right.

By faith in Christ we hear the promise:
you, O Lord, will heal; you will love. Amen

Tekoa

Amos 1:1; 5:21-24
*Amos was among the shepherds of Tekoa
two years before the earthquake.*

Tekoa. No one would pay attention to this town south of Bethlehem if it were not connected with the prophet Amos. No one would remember that it ever existed had not Amos received his call there. This call of God astounded him, since he was, he said, "no prophet, nor a prophet's son; but . . . a herdsman, and a dresser of sycamore trees" (7:14). There in the loneliness, along the sheep trails, he heard the call of the Lord to prophecy.

Tekoa. Here we are reminded that the call of God can come to the most unexpected people in the least remarkable places. It can come to people like us, in places like ours, as ordinary as we and these may be.

This day and tomorrow, as we put a hand to staff or plow or knife or pen, literally or figuratively; as we face computer or cradle, factory bench or classroom, unemployment line or sickbed, we are in readiness to be called. That call does not come through thunder or earthquake or a voice from heaven, but through the beckonings of people in need and through our own vision of opportunity to serve God.

Most of what Amos said had to be directed against people in power. But if Amos preached "against," God also gave him a message "for" Israel and us. At once a threat and a promise, the word insists that God will effect justice—and for those made just in Christ and empowered by him to serve justice, that bodes well.

*Lord, interrupt our thoughtless routines with your word of judgment,
and then in grace let righteousness flow. Amen*

Nineveh

Jonah 1:1-2; 4:6-11
And should I not be concerned about Nineveh, that great city?

Nineveh. That great city is so like the cities of our time. The mention of Nineveh calls to mind any place that is great, ungovernable, inhumane—and far from God. These cities—and towns too, for that matter—stand under judgment. So do ours.

It would be easy to write them off, to be unconcerned about them, to let them go their own way while we carve out little corners where we can pursue spiritual safety. Before we do so, however, Nineveh and its story deserve a second look.

The writer of the book of Jonah described Nineveh most memorably. With the mind of an atlas-writer he noted that it took a journey of three days, a long walk, to cross this urban center. This metropolis was doomed, and Jonah was to be the voice of its doom. The prophet did everything he could to evade the call of God to pronounce judgment, but in the end he did preach. Then, to his almost horrified surprise, "the people of Nineveh believed God" (3:5). They proclaimed a fast.

In a delightful literary touch, we read that "God changed his mind" and spared Nineveh (3:10). This change is again astonishing, as surprising as the fact that Jonah, who should have known better, could not welcome this divine grace and mercy. The pettiness of a prophet gave the writer the chance to say that the God who shows concern is gracious and spares the repentant. In ancient cities and today, God spares us.

God of grace, help us to rejoice in the fortunes
that replace misfortunes among the wicked who repent,
and lead us to good new fortunes and destinies. Amen

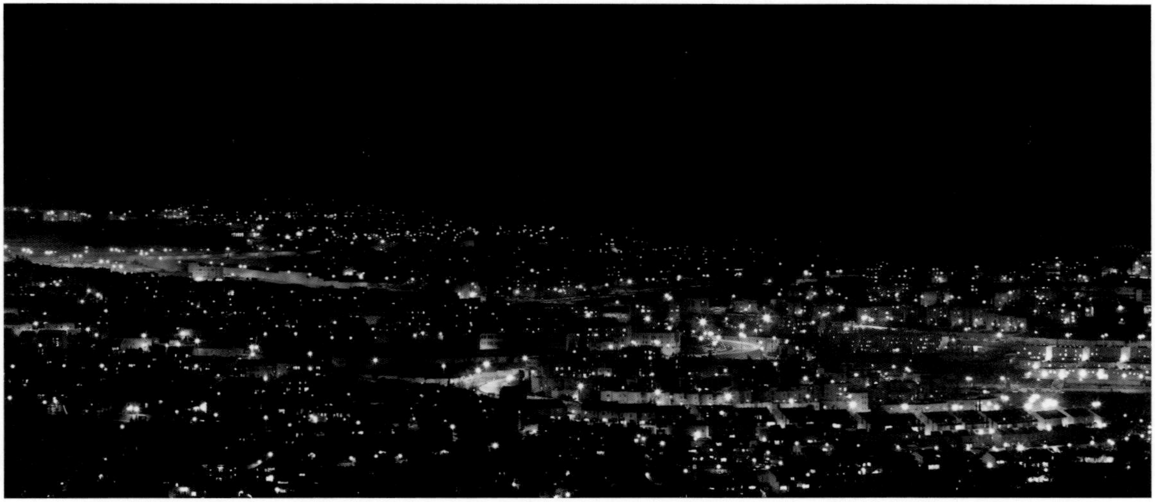

Bethlehem

Micah 4:3-5; 5:1-5

But you, O Bethlehem of Ephrathah, who are one of the little clans of Judah, from you shall one come forth.

Bethlehem, as in "O Little Town of . . . ," is one of the most familiar names along the pilgrim walk. Jesus was born in a town with that name. The Gospel writers connect that birthplace with the Bethlehem mentioned by the prophet Micah.

Micah, centuries before, was expecting salvation for Israel. He wanted to train Israel's eyes and his own to look for help to come from unexpected places. People in Micah's time expected leadership to come from important places and through people of power. People today expect leadership to come from important places and through people of power. People naturally do natural things and expect the expectable.

The prophets and evangelists, however, full of the Holy Spirit, turn around all of these expectations. No one did that more dramatically than Micah, who had visions of a future when people would "walk in the name of the Lord our God." He started talking about people as humble as a shepherd king becoming an agent of God.

Where did Micah look for rescue? This ruler, he said, would come from nowhere, or almost nowhere. Then he pronounced the obscure name: Bethlehem. Jesus came from Bethlehem, "and he shall be the one of peace" in a world that needs it and in our heart where he will find a home.

Train our eyes to find your doings, O Lord, in out-of-the-way places and to see you at work in the hands and voices of people who seem weak. Amen

Thebes

Nahum 3:8-13
Are you better than Thebes that sat by the Nile?
You will go into hiding; you will seek a refuge from the enemy.

Thebes, a city by the Nile. In what were news events very long ago, Assyria had taken Thebes captive, and now Assyria was about to be destroyed. Once again our spiritual journey takes us to a place in the stone piles and rubble of ancient Egypt, where very contemporary points get made.

On only this day of the pilgrimage we hear a prophecy tempered with no softness, a word of judgment unmixed with mercy, spoken against a people who evidently experienced no mercy. In isolation it presents images that are too stark; we may have to turn back a page or two for comforting messages to sustain us through the day. But we will not evade this one.

The life of the believer is never one of all softness, mercy, and sweetness. We use the season of pilgrimage to relearn how serious is the call of a holy God, how high the standards, how sacred the passion, how full of regard for the victims of oppression the Divine One has to be.

So we read lines of Nahum to face God's judgment. Nahum is an angry editorial writer, working as if in a spirit of revenge against national enemies. In a superb, vivid poem, Nahum spells out the Lord's judgment on a corrupt, rebellious other nation.

So, with mixed feelings, we will respond to Nahum's message by recognizing that pride and defiance in our world and heart have to give way to humility and love. God is merciful, as we are not, and thus this God names a people to which we want to belong, a people "better than Thebes."

In the fall of empires, O God, help us to see your hand. In the peace of the cities where your righteousness prevails, let us find security. Amen

Mount Paran

Habakkuk 3:3; 2:1-4
God, who came from Mount Paran, said,
"There is still a vision for the appointed time. Wait for it."

Mount Paran. This is Mount Sinai, now with a different name. The prophet Habakkuk experienced the revealing of God from such a high place. The word of what he saw and heard reaches across the ages.

Habakkuk would be at home in our world and he speaks to our heart. He asks our questions. He might well have written the book *Why Bad Things Happen to Good People*, though he never would have pretended to provide a fully satisfying answer to the question. One commentary on the book of Habakkuk has its theme right. It is called *The Eternal Why.*

Habakkuk asks with us and for us why evil ones prosper at the expense of innocents. God provides what has to sound like an unsatisfying answer. Habakkuk asks again, and this time at least receives a promise for the future.

Who among those that we know will get through, or got through, this day without having some moments of asking *why* about urgent puzzles? None who are thoughtful. But those who identify with Habakkuk often have been inspired to remain with their causes and stay with their hope in the light of God's second answer, which is one of hope. They build their buildings in what had been waste places and keep lights burning against the surrounding darkness. The word in this prophecy bears repeating often through the next hours: "For there is still a vision for the appointed time; it speaks of the end, and does not lie. If it seems to tarry, wait for it; it will surely come, it will not delay." It will surely come.

We know, O Lord, that you will keep your promises. In faith we commend our day to your care. Teach us patience and keep the vision of you before us. Amen

Gaza

Zephaniah 2:4-7
*For Gaza shall be deserted. The seacoast shall become
the possession of the remnant of the house of Judah.*

Gaza. The city near the sea was, in ancient times, a place of power. Like so many others, it would be laid waste. The prophet knew that and said so.

Who cares and why care now? We and the people around us face our own intractable problems, and the front pages and prime-time television bring word of more than we can handle. Small personal issues are nagging, troubling. Suddenly we are called to pay attention to this ancient city. We find ourselves asking what message there can be for us in a story from the world of Zephaniah, about whom we know nothing.

Then come thoughts like these: sometimes we use too modest a canvas, too small a screen, on which to paint or project the pictures that guide life today. The point of it all: our life and times make best sense when viewed against the background of the just activity of God.

A Jewish atheist novelist claimed that the people of Israel invented a just God. Thus their Lord would devastate enemies like Assyria, Egypt, and Gaza. But the inventors were consistent and devised a God who surprised them by being consistent. This God held his own people to higher standards than those used to measure or punish their enemies!

The novelist was wrong about the inventing, but not about the consistency. Zephaniah, however, like so many prophets, noted that the same God who must leave Gaza desolate will create secure places for shepherds and flocks and, by extension, safe refuges for those who welcome them. The promise said that the humble of the land who seek the Lord would become a faithful remnant among the people and God would be mindful of them—as God will be mindful of us in the Gaza, the desolation that surrounds us, our place, our path.

*God who was mindful of the remnant in Israel,
now look on us and ours and our neighbors and,
on Christ's account, be mindful of us and grant us peace. Amen*

Bethel

Zechariah 7:2, 8-14; 8:1-8
The people of Bethel had sent men to entreat the favor of the Lord.

Bethel. This place gets two visits. Pages and days ago its image was the ladder that figured in Jacob's vision of heaven. This second time on the same pilgrimage it is a major city, both a shrine and a crossroads. The people of this place came to the prophet Zechariah to ask a rather technical question about how to observe a fast. This may not be on our mind today, but the rest of the lines describe a future that is.

Zechariah answered the people of Bethel in the name of the Lord. God had wanted them to "render true judgments, show kindness and mercy to one another" and not to "oppress the widow, the orphan, the alien, or the poor." The people disobeyed, and their land was left desolate. It must have looked like the cities around us when widows, orphans, aliens, and the poor get abandoned.

The God who spoke to and through Zechariah did not leave Bethel and Zion desolate. God announced a gracious, delightful, even springtime vision that might inspire work for a better human scene today: "Old men and old women shall again sit in the streets of Jerusalem. . . . And the streets of the city shall be full of boys and girls playing in its streets."

Boys and girls playing in the streets, away from the guns of gang warfare and other jeopardies. Such a vision, across a generation gap and in the aftermath of desolation, counters and replaces those that go with loss, when both rustbelt and farmbelt deny hopes and cities are unsafe. As for the old and young everywhere, God then announced and now announces, "They shall be my people and I will be their God, in faithfulness and in righteousness."

Keep before us today, O Lord, a picture of safety and carefreeness
which you offer in Christ, as we learn to serve
your purposes for our place and time. Amen

Judah

Malachi 3:1-4
***Then the offering of Judah and Jerusalem will be pleasing to the Lord
as in the days of old and as in former years.***

Judah. The name of a man became the name of a tribe, and in turn it then became the name of one part of God's people.

On the second-to-last page of the Old Testament, and on this the last day of what has been the prophetic part of our spiritual journey, a word about Judah becomes the word that will mark our night and day: fire!

Leading up to the fire, we hear that God will send "the messenger of the covenant in whom you delight." This recalls to our ear the voice in Handel's *Messiah:* "But who can endure the day of his coming? For he is like a refiner's fire . . . and he will purify."

Our way of living and thinking needs and we now welcome purifying fires, wanting the blights and mars to disappear. We belong in a company of people who have become corrupted and we are demoralized. Help comes: a "messenger of the covenant," a speaker of the divine word, will bring both judgment and delight, and some of that coming will be apparent this day and tomorrow.

Otherwise estranged from God, we link up with Judah and Jerusalem in their act of bringing offerings that will be pleasing to the Lord. We offer day and night and all our doings. Christians read these verses in Malachi in the light of Jesus' word about John the Baptist, the messenger who prepared his way. With all these layers of meaning at hand, we hear both Malachi and John and rise to follow, in their light, walking the rest of the way with Jesus.

*Purify and refine us in the fires of your word, Lord God,
bringing the message of a renewed covenant, of acceptable offerings,
of a grace that makes purifying possible. Amen*

Nazareth

Luke 1:26-38
*In the sixth month the angel Gabriel was sent by God
to a town in Galilee called Nazareth, to a virgin.*

Nazareth is the locale for the event we call the annunciation, when Gabriel told Mary she would be the mother of the Messiah. Christians celebrate the occasion every March 25, nine months before they celebrate Christmas. But the encounter between the Word, through the angel, and the young virgin of Nazareth deserves thought any day of any year. It is an alert that helps us reflect on how God surprises humans and how in faith believers respond.

A prayer for the festival of the Annunciation joins this day with days marked by death and resurrection, connecting beginnings and endings of a story: "Pour your grace into our hearts, O Lord," it says, "that we, who have known the incarnation of your Son, Jesus Christ, announced by an angel, may by his cross and Passion be brought to the glory of his resurrection . . . " (*LBW*, p. 32).

Who cares *when* in the year we hear of an angel announcing a conception to Mary, a birth to shepherds, an empty tomb to women? There is reason to care, however, that every day the benefits of all the announcements work their effect in the world. Each such announcement, we know, has a bearing on our life this day, on the path of the one "called Son of God."

Rivers of ink have been spilled on the issue of this announcement and of a virgin birth. Let such rivers flow. For us the issue is, what does its story tell us about the response of faith? The figure of Mary means many things. Today we will let her be the model of how we should react in faith: in the hours ahead, waking or sleeping, we will be guided by a response that lets things happen according to the will and word and love of God. Nothing that will happen then need divert us and fellow pilgrims from this march of faith in daily life.

*Most High God, help us join Mary in being servants of the Lord.
Let it be with us also according to your word,
whatever that word for today might be. Help us listen for it. Amen*

Cana

John 2:1-12
*Jesus and his disciples had been invited
to a wedding in Cana of Galilee.*

Cana. The last thing one would expect to be appropriate during a solemn pilgrimage is a visit to a rousing party at a wedding. Yet surprises occur on the best-kept calendars. They interrupt the best-planned schedules. They punctuate even the most set ways of life. We propose the course of a day and Jesus gets in the way and changes our idea of how it is to be pursued.

With good reason we want to linger at Cana, to capture the conversations and be caught up in the party mood. We have time to look around in all the confusion. A small detail: there are some stone water jars. The Gospel adds an important touch: the water is "for the Jewish rites of purification." As important as that water and those rites have been, they are to be replaced by something new.

That something new, here as several times along the way, is named new wine. But clearly the new wine is not in the story only because of its "sign"— water turned into wine!—as something miraculous to drink. That original wine disappeared in one evening. The new wine is a signal that something new is here to stay. Here is something that replaces the old rite. We get to sit at the banquet table with Jesus and his party. There is no need to turn back to the old means of purification. Cana is a party, but it has turned into a revelation. We will revel in it in the hours ahead.

*Lord, help us greet the new, the replacement for the things
to which we have clung with the best of intentions. Let us enjoy the company
at the banquet of life that you grace with your presence. Amen*

Capernaum

Mark 2:1-12
When Jesus returned to Capernaum, many gathered there.
Afterwards they glorified God, saying,
"We have never seen anything like this!"

Capernaum is a village we like to visit because it was the favored town of Jesus. No journey of faith could bypass that pleasant settlement on the shores of Galilee. On pilgrimage we are anything but tourists, but there are tourists here, too. They come to a synagogue that quite likely replaces one on the exact spot where Jesus spoke.

The Capernaum in our mind's eye is serene. But it was also the scene of many shocks. In one of the stories, people came to Jesus bearing a paralyzed man whom they wanted to have healed. Jesus greeted them with a startling announcement whose effects still quicken us.

Now, as then, we bring Jesus our problems, our ills. He diagnoses what really ails us and says, "Your sins are forgiven." Like people in the old story, we have a different name for what is bothering us. We bring an ailment as we have diagnosed it and challenge God to make a difference. In the name of God, Jesus diagnoses a different malady and provides a cure for our misplaced priorities and for what was really plaguing.

When Jesus says, "Your sins are forgiven," he is giving us a life of health. With the barriers removed between us and a holy God, we are free to meet the challenges and receive the gifts of the day.

Let us, O Lord, hear the word that places us in the company of the forgiven and free, and help us to receive it in trust. Amen

The Sea of Galilee

Mark 3:7-12

***Jesus departed to the sea, and hearing all that he was doing,
a great multitude followed him.***

Galilee. "The sea," the Gospels usually call it. We know it as a small lake that plays a large part in Jesus' story and in ours. We have in imagination visited it in calm and in storms and know it as a place where Jesus called the disciples, went fishing, rested, and taught.

Today, he teaches. The years that have passed and the miles that separate us from the waters do not prevent us from receiving what the first disciples and the original crowds from Judah, Jerusalem, and elsewhere received. We join those who get to hear "all that he was doing." We can take a moment this hour, this day, to close our eyes and picture him speaking from the boat in which he took refuge, the craft that he made his pulpit. His voice sounds to people on the shore, us among them.

So what is this? What is "all that he is doing" in our lives as we follow his on this journey? Those on pilgrimage become more aware each day that the pace is picking up at each stop, even at this quiet one. Quiet? Here, now, is the voice of multitudes.

All that Jesus was doing, is doing, will come to a climax when he gives himself on the cross. Here already he shares his healing powers, utters his commands, provides his consoling words, and gives guidance in messages we hear afresh from the speaker in the boat.

*Speak today, Lord. We are eager to hear you tell what you have done
and are doing now and what this means for our calling. Amen*

Sychar

John 4:5-15
Jesus came to Jacob's well at Sychar.
A Samaritan woman came there to draw water.

Sychar. Another place that is not on present-day maps. Tourist guides like to point to a well they call Jacob's Well and say, "This is it." Any well will do, however, for it is the water and not the wood and stone surrounding it or the rope and bucket that dip into it about which we are to think at this stop.

The story about the well is familiar: Jesus asks for water from a Samaritan, and thus an alien. She puzzles that any Jewish man would "share things in common" with her, a Samaritan, a woman. We picture her with head and shoulders bowed from the weight of many carryings of water, her legs weary from her many trudges up the hill to home. She is thirsty, really thirsty, eager for any pure water that will soothe her throat and refresh her body.

Jesus tells her that he could give her "living water." This only puzzles her further. Jacob, her ancestor, drank of this well and had to be content with the water as it was. Is this stranger greater than the great Jacob, who with his flocks drank from the well?

Jesus distanced himself from the ordinary waters that ordinary people drank on ordinary days; he was not talking about anything like that. "Those who drink of the water that I will give them will never be thirsty," he can say, for this water "will become in them a spring of water gushing up to eternal life."

Sir, give us this water, so that we may never be thirsty, sustained as we will be
by the refreshment you bring, the refreshment you are. Amen

Caesarea Philippi

Mark 8:27-30
*Jesus went on to the villages of Caesarea Philippi
and asked his disciples, "Who do people say that I am?"*

Caesarea Philippi stands for the place, or places, where disciples take a stand. Caesar Augustus is gone with all the Caesars. Herod Philip is gone with all the Herods. Therefore Caesarea Philippi, which combines the names, belongs to history. Let it lie.

Jesus the Christ, who witnessed in the villages there, lives today and towers above those who witness to him.

Pilgrimages are for walkers, yet for the moment we stand in this company of witnesses. Along the way we get pulled aside for a test of identity, a statement of stammered convictions.

Today we are asked, as so often, who are you? To whom do you belong? Who gets your loyalty? Answers to such questions call forth reference to families, clubs, churches, races, or nations. But this time the question about identity asks about our attitude to someone else. Jesus: "Who do people say that I am?" The question haunts and challenges us as it did disciples long ago. If we answer in faith, we come to know who we are, to whom we belong.

When Jesus asked brusquely, "Who do people say that I am?" the disciples offered, as we might have, three wrong answers and then Peter spoke the right one: "You are the Messiah," the one anointed by God. We know this and become part of his movement. That is how our life takes shape today, under the beckoning cross.

Going ahead of our companions and us on this walk to Jerusalem is the Messiah, the one God anointed to lead the walk. At its end, he will give his very life. He has empowered us and all who follow to see him as the Anointed One. We become one with the stumbling but hope-filled insiders as we follow.

*Embolden us to find opportunities to state convictions about who you are
and what you do for all, O Lord, and keep us steadfast. Amen*

Mount Tabor

Luke 9:28-36
Jesus went up on the mountain to pray.
And the appearance of his face changed.

Mount Tabor. We will call this high point Mount Tabor. The Bible does not name the place, but at times it is convenient to follow tradition and tourist guides when fixing an image in the mind. On the other hand, any mountain in one's imagination will do for recalling what happens.

This craggy, brilliant stop seems out of place, at least for a moment, to anyone following Jesus in his march to Jerusalem and the cross. These are days for shadows, spectres, darknesses. Now, suddenly, here is an event called Jesus' "transfiguration." According to the stories, his face and figure were changed. His clothes, again according to Luke, became "dazzling white," as they were to be in his resurrection.

How ever shall we endure such brightness, such luster, in the shadows of this journey to Jerusalem and its cross? What will become of the symbolic sackcloth and ashes our soul should wear, if we get too close to the dazzling aura of Jesus? If this is to be a serious pilgrimage with him, will not this moment on a mountaintop breed illusion and confusion?

We get answers: we endure and enjoy the brightness because our eyes remain eager for a vision of the glorious Lord whose light is never completely hidden. Sackcloth and ashes are not the only wardrobe and cosmetics to be worn when we are on a journey that is already touched by Jesus' light. This is no diversion or interruption at all. It is a God-planned part of the pilgrimage. In it we see and in its story we hear the promise of the God of light.

Three witnesses on the scene speak for us: today "it is good for us to be here," to be astonished by the voice from above bidding, "This is my Son, my Chosen; listen to him!"

God of light, we join those who look for signs of the glory,
and we listen for the sounds of endorsement.
Graced anew, we can readily face the darkness that still threatens. Amen

Samaria

Luke 9:51-56
***On their way they entered a village of the Samaritans,
but the Samaritans did not receive Jesus.***

Samaria had a terrible reputation among the people around Jesus. It was a district Jews from the north avoided on their way to Jerusalem. In turn—people and peoples are like that—Samaritans rejected Jews on their pilgrim ways.

Samaria. Here the disciples wanted to prepare a place to stay. But there was no stopping here, because Jesus' "face was set toward Jerusalem."

We know figurative Samarias well these days. The front page tells of Samaritan-like sects and tribes who reject each other. They build walls and then block the openings. Fences and barbed wire keep people apart. Some days we wish their bickering and fighting would stop; we would shout "Enough!" We hear the religiously impatient in effect ask, as disciples did once upon a time, that Jesus "command fire to come down . . . and consume" those with whom they differ. Instead Jesus scolds the impatient and takes them "to another village" along the way. We will walk with them.

Samaria and what it represents are distractions from the purposes Jesus has in mind. His face set toward Jerusalem is a face focused where we need to focus. If our life seems ordinary and our place in history small, still we can picture how Jesus felt. We hate to be rejected or turned away from our intentions. He had more reason to be hurt. But his purpose remained clear. So, moved by love, he pressed on toward a hill, to his cross.

Because of that cross and what goes with it we find acceptance by God. Obstacles and snubs are insignificant in the face of such a reality. Awareness of the divine purpose in the great and small events of life guides the day. During it, God keeps accepting people like us. Accepting us.

*We are grateful, Lord, that we get to receive Christ and to follow him,
undeterred, ready for the path, for whatever lies ahead. Amen*

Jericho

Mark 10:46-52
They came to Jericho. A blind beggar was sitting by the roadside.

Jericho is a last stop along the way before the ancient story moves to the villages east of Jerusalem and then to Jerusalem itself. There Jesus will be killed. On this way, crowds gather. Here at Jericho the call of a blind beggar disturbs the plot of the story; he upsets the crowd with his plea. Each of us has a plot figured out for this day or the next, but we know it will be disrupted by strangers along the way. They have their needs, too.

If we are physically blind and hear stories like this read, we identify with the beggar at once. If we are sighted and read them ourselves, we have to work harder to show empathy. And then it occurs to us: in the important things, in matters that go beyond the physical, *we are one of the blind!* Our eyes weaken as we see too many bright things of the world. They dull because our mind neglects the sharpness of the divine vision. They distort, they blur, they fail.

Here at Jericho everyone is on equal terms. The cry of the heart, then, is again, "Son of David, have mercy on me!" Now, as then, the quieting word of Jesus comes to change the day: "Take heart."

"Let me see again." That blind man's credible request becomes ours. We seek new vision. We identify with the beggar. There is no question but that the story in Mark tells of a wondrous happening, a real restoring of sight.

There is also no question but that the story in Mark gets lived out today when we hear, in respect to whatever ails, limits, or confines us, "Your faith has made you well." Jesus speaks it afresh.

Lord, that we may receive our sight again, after the blindness that has come upon us and the blindness we have chosen: we ask your mercy. Amen

The Bethany Tomb

John 11:1-45
Jesus said to her, "I am the resurrection and the life."

Bethany. This village seems to be a dead end, with the accent on "dead." Can a spiritual pilgrimage avoid death, ends, darkness? If the journey of the soul follows the map of experience, we cannot evade the sight of gaping tombs.

Here lay Lazarus, a dear friend. With Jesus away, he died, was shrouded and entombed. That the death meant separation, as all death does, is clear from the fact that Jesus wept, as a good friend would do, upon hearing that Lazarus was gone.

At the end of the story Jesus bid Lazarus to come forth, an early sign of the new creation, one of many miracles his critics knew he was doing.

For us today, though, it is the middle of the story that helps. Martha, the sister of Lazarus, confronted Jesus with tears, only to hear that her brother would "rise again." Martha, with good head knowledge, gave the proper doctrinal answer she must have learned from the rabbis: she knew that her brother would rise again. But she said it in comfortless spirit, between apathy and despair, drawing no hope from the knowledge.

So Jesus did what Jesus does for us today. He announces what happens in his presence: "I am the resurrection and the life." Those who believe in him, "even though they die, will live." In fact, living and believing in him we "will never die." That we will die does not make Jesus a deceiver. He helps us look at living, dying, and living in new ways. God in Christ is with us on the bright walks of life and in the darkness with which the earth surrounds or covers us in ordinary death. And through it all, while imparting the light that never goes out, God in Christ is with us as the life that continues through our pilgrimage and beyond.

*Resurrection and life that you are, guide us to use
the knowledge we already have until we come to the hope that we crave
and the faith that we need along this way. Amen*

Bethphage

Matthew 21:1-9
***When they had come near Jerusalem and had reached Bethphage,
Jesus sent two disciples.***

Bethphage. This village is out of sight but not out of mind. That is, no one knows where it was. It evidently did not count for much even in Jesus' time. Bethphage was just another forgettable place along the road Jesus took near Bethany, above Jerusalem, on the way to his death. Yet there is good reason for us to stop here, to pause and imagine.

Bethphage matters because it stands for all the places where people like us get chances to be a part of Jesus' purposes. At stopping places and moments like this we get to participate in the divine doings that would save the world.

Bethphage was part of the drama on a Sunday that we call Palm Sunday. On that day, as today, believers get to greet Jesus in song and prayer, in bread and wine, in listening to the Word and in Christian conversation. Symbolically and sometimes actually they wave palms. Any day, any place, Bethphage can signal a call to sing hosannas, to live with a day of praise.

Palm-waving and hosanna-shouting create a stir, but before they occur, God asks for little, apparently unimportant, things to be done. Just as Jesus went from Bethphage displaying a mixture of triumph and humility, glory and weakness, he comes in the midst of confusion today. The little things we get to do are part of the excitement. Bethphage brings recall of obedient disciples who went ahead to carry out small tasks, like renting a donkey. We hear of no grumbling this day: "The disciples went and did as Jesus had directed them." Their quiet response inspires ours today and lets us see significance in the ordinary.

*Graced as we are to participate in your divine doings, O Lord,
give us the vision to see the importance of small tasks. Amen*

Jerusalem

Matthew 23:37–24:2
*Jerusalem, Jerusalem, how often have I desired to gather
your children together as a hen gathers her brood.*

Jerusalem figures positively in the imagination of any pilgrim along the way. So it seems unfair to that city for us to stop and think about its meaning immediately after Jesus has spoken his most sad word about it.

For all the positive images this holy city brings, we recall that Jesus often has to speak prophetically against it. Jerusalem even "kills the prophets and stones those who are sent to it!" In many ways, our fellow citizens and we do the same, and no one notices. We find ourselves not wanting to think of the tears of Jesus or the warnings.

Jesus says he often wanted to gather and protect the citizens. His call still comes, to people on farms, in towns, in today's Jerusalems. It is easy to ignore the call, to be distracted, to avoid him. The city, for all its crowding, lets us be isolated; it permits us to think we can be uncommitted, can quietly go along with acts of evil. Jesus cried out and cried in this story of Jerusalem. Still he weeps.

We need more than his tears to get us through this day, this night. Shall we flee to the sanctuary, turning our back on the city?

Jerusalem boasted a sanctuary, a temple, but Jesus said that even it would be destroyed. The temples around us are erected for worship: of God, money, the pleasures of life, the rites of the nation. Not all the uses of these temples work against the purposes of God, but all can be "thrown down." In the next twenty-four hours, whatever we do can be a part of rebuilding in the midst of distraction and destruction. The promise remains: there is refuge in the company of the children of the city, gathered for the protection promised today. The children are not innocents, but God favors them since they cannot protect themselves. Nor could we, without divine care.

We would be in the company of those you gather, O Lord;
let us not resist the call or forget your tears.
In this company is the city of refuge for our souls. Amen

The Mount of Olives

Matthew 24:3-14
*When he was sitting on the Mount of Olives,
the disciples came to him privately.*

The Mount of Olives. Many mountains rise above and surround the paths along the way with Jesus. Some are remote, but this one, the Mount of Olives, is a public place from which Jesus entered Jerusalem, bidding those close to him to come along.

This day, however, it comes to mind as a private place. Its quiet is interrupted by a startling conversation on which we get to eavesdrop. What we overhear as Jesus talks with the disciples who had climbed this mount with him and who huddle under the olive trees is shocking. Even in the places apart, the God who visits the world in Jesus jolts the complacent. That God enters ordinary lives with talk about the drama of that day, but he talks also about this day. Not all of the words sound like "good news" of the sort that gets called gospel.

This Mount of Olives becomes the locale where we hear warnings that still color life: that many would lead others astray; that "nation will rise against nation," as the morning news tells that they still do; that there must be birthpangs while the new kingdom is coming. We hear Jesus saying, through tears, that he knows not all will be faithful and "the love of many will grow cold." Will ours?

Jesus foresees what has happened for centuries: straying, alarm, pangs, torture, hatred, betrayal, lawlessness, and coldness. These need not be the spiritual fate of those who believe, for in the company of others who listen on this tree-marked mountainside we hear that in his care there is assurance. The one "who endures to the end will be saved."

*The good news: Lord, let it be proclaimed in public and let it reach
the private corners of our minds and hearts; give us grace to endure. Amen*

Bethany

Matthew 26:6-13
While Jesus was at Bethany, a woman came to him with
an alabaster jar of very costly ointment, and she poured it on his head.

Bethany. This place is familiar as a village we have visited before, a village where friends of Jesus lived. This time it is a resting place along Jesus' way, and along our way it figures in the imagination as a spiritual resting place.

Bethany. Here is the house of Simon the leper. Simon is host to Jesus, who is on his path to an upper room for a last supper, and on to Golgotha, and finally to a garden with a grave in it, for him.

Perhaps at Bethany there is the mild stench of decayed leper's limbs, for the world then, as now, was marked by disease. But the stench is offset by the fragrance of incense and odors of supper foods.

A woman is doing something shocking: as she pours out expensive oil to anoint Jesus, we hear him say, "She has prepared me for burial." She, not Peter, not James, not John, not any appointed man, but "the woman" has prepared him and acted for everyone who cares.

Why waste a minute of this day rehearsing the argument of those disciples who griped that her costly ointment was a waste? Better to spend the hours remembering that Jesus called the story of this event, "this good news," a story that would be told "in the whole world."

We belong to that world and hunger for good news. We remember in reverence the woman and now join in her intentions, hoping to make her ointment and her act our own. Now, strangely, it is "good news" to hear of a body prepared for burial.

O Lord, in remembrance of her, an anointing woman, help us find new resolve to
be generous participants in your ways and works. Amen

Gethsemane

Matthew 26:36-46
Then Jesus went with them to a place called Gethsemane.
He went away and prayed.

Gethsemane. This "oil press"—for that is what the name means—is an estate across a brook and low on a mountain, the place where we eavesdrop and over-hear Jesus praying a day before his death.

We would never compare our Gethsemanes to his, but we have ours, where prayer comes in agony. So we listen closely to him. The sleepy disciples represent us well most of the time, for we can often ignore the divine agony and let things take their course. But we are trained to be alert, to be close to the one who in this garden "threw himself on the ground and prayed."

Since this betrayed Son of Man is the one in whom God acts freely and richly toward us, there are good reasons for us to learn and reflect on his mental state and his prayer.

"My Father, . . . not what I want but what you want." Jesus has already taught the prayer that asks of God that "your will be done." But here we note that he does not gasp the prayer and give up in defeat against an overpowering will of God. Instead he keeps on praying, three times, and never in resignation. Finally, back to the disciples: "Get up, let us be going." Alert, now, we follow.

"Get up, let us be going" remains the call for today, from under the gnarled olive trees or in the midst of the city. We will never forget that after Jesus commends himself to God's will, he keeps on praying, keeps on convers-ing, staying close. So will we.

We pray, and pray, and pray "your will be done,"
O Lord, and safely resting in that will, prepare to go on,
no matter what is ahead. Amen

Golgotha

Matthew 27:32-37
*When they came to a place called Golgotha
(which means Place of a Skull), they crucified him.*

Golgotha. The throat of the thoughtful believer gags, and the tongue finds it hard even to say the name of this place. Golgotha is a site beyond the walls, but at the crossroads. We think of it as being either in one of the finer suburbs or at the city dump: God meets people at extreme points. Golgotha was a place of executions. We push it from our memory, the way we try to forget the electric chair and Death Row. But against our will, Golgotha presses itself on our mind.

Here "they" executed Jesus. "They"—it is always "they"—denied love, spit against justice, were violent against the gentle, pit vileness against perfection, and gave hate an apparent victory over love.

Who are "they"? Peter, who denied the love? Crowds who spit? Taunters who were violent? Passersby who were vile?

This is the hour to take away the question marks, the day to stop pointing fingers at others. Non-Jews long blamed Jews, and rivers of blood issued from their despicable charges. Moderns blame ancient Romans, for whom no one speaks up today. The accusing finger that points, we note, is curved; it turns back on the one who accuses. "We" made Golgotha necessary.

Golgotha is the symbolic site for every act in which we banish Christ from our life. Yet Golgotha, the "place of a skull," also signals that the victory of hate over love was only apparent, only temporary. Here and now God refuses to let the divine love be denied by our denials, to let the divine reach be ignored or repudiated. We will know that love today.

*Lord God, we, identified as being among those who crucify Christ,
rejoice to be identified with those who are drawn near to you by his self-giving. Amen*

A Tomb in Jerusalem

Matthew 27:57-61
So Joseph laid the body in his own new tomb,
which he had hewn in the rock.

A tomb in Jerusalem. Here, after the death of Jesus and of hope, one would expect the trail to end. Every day, every turning of the page so far, has pointed to another that would follow. This time the visit to places along the way ends in the vision and the recall of this scene of death. So one would think, if this were an ordinary recall of an ordinary plot, of a life like all others.

A stark and menacing tomb in Jerusalem it is. But as we think of it, a different reality changes everything. Unfortunately for those who like suspense in their stories, this one gets spoiled because almost everyone knows that another chapter will follow. In this plot, the tomb is like a stage prop, needed for one day, to be emptied of the crucified body just placed there. Fortunately for those, like us, who want to live and who go on doing so day by day, we already know what the next page, the next day, will mean.

We will not, however, hurry past this tomb in Jerusalem. Today its image will cross our mind often, signaling the bleakness that took over the minds of hope-less disciples and that threatens us when we act as if a sealed tomb ends the story of life.

In the hours of a day like this we will admire the Josephs—one loaned his tomb—who still show respect for Jesus. We will weep with the Marys who kept a vigil by the rock-closed grave. And while doing so, we will identify with their sense of abandonment, so like our own, experienced whenever the presence of God is missing. The eye of faith sees even in the darkness of such hours that God is present and that abandonment is not the last word.

Stay with us and ours and all, loving and careful one,
through the vigil of this day and the night to come,
after which there is no more night. Amen

Galilee

Matthew 28:1-10
"He is going ahead of you to Galilee; there you will see him."
This is my message for you.

Galilee represents the end of this pathway. It names the place where those who followed Jesus were to see him again, now that he was raised to new life. Now Galilee can represent the many meeting places where he greets believers, including us.

Galilee, a land ruled by kings named Herod, was a territory made up largely of villages. Stories of the times Jesus spent here in his boyhood and much of his ministry remain vivid. It was an ordinary place. Here Jesus promised to meet disciples after he rose from death, and here he did. It is an extraordinary place. It is vivid in believers' minds, and we focus ours here today.

Once a year the minds of all believers celebrate this place, on Easter. But when the trumpets of Easter morning have quieted and its lilies have drooped and disappeared, the story of the risen Jesus still sounds, faith is enlivened, hope reappears.

The name *Galilee* remains on maps; its villages beckon tourists. But far more important is what it signals: that every day is an Easter, a festival of resurrection; that every place can become a Galilee where Jesus greets believers and walks with them.

We have followed the call and invitation of God from the stories of the first creation to these stories of the new creation. Each sunset the risen Jesus Christ imparts peace and calms the heart. Each sunrise God in Christ is here to lead the journey of our ordinary days, making them all, including this one, extraordinary. The new creation has begun. We are part of it, receiving its gifts, and we are free to put them to work. In the Galilee of the heart and the mind, we will not walk alone.

In the paths of a figurative Galilee and the pathways of our real life,
meet us in grace, risen Lord, and let us be part of the new creation. Amen

Notes on the Photographs

Although most of the photographs in *Places Along the Way* were taken between 1992 and 1994 in Israel and Egypt, most were not taken at the site named. There are three reasons for this.

—No one knows the actual site or the site doesn't exist in a fashion capable of being photographed. (Many locations ascribed by "tradition" were designated centuries after the life of Jesus and subsequently covered with modern shrines.)

—The same factors that give many places their religious significance also preserve them as areas of political tension thousands of years later, making visits there—let alone photography!—difficult or dangerous.

—The pictures are intended to be evocative rather than descriptive, inspiring "impressions" rather than providing guidebook-like "portraits." Merely suggesting the essence of the place or story allows you, the reader, to fill in the details through personal interpretation and meditation.

—Micah Marty

Frontispiece *(page 2)* – For centuries, Christians have traveled to the Holy Land, building churches like this one in Capernaum to mark places associated with the faith story.

Author's Introduction *(page 6)* – Countless pilgrims setting out on spiritual journeys have entered through this door to St. Catherine's Monastery, at the foot of Mount Sinai.

Photographer's Introduction *(page 8)* – We begin journeys with a sense of anticipation; we may have a direction in mind, but we are open to unexpected opportunities.

One Day, One Page *(page 10)* – Although we may take different paths, we find that we share a common direction.

Chaos *(page 13)* – How does one illustrate something that is "without form"? How do we envision the chaos, the universal sea of darkness, out of which a bright earth was created?

Eden *(page 14)* – While gardens are usually human arrangements subject to different tastes, the perfection of creation might best be seen in a single blossom. We find in the bee a symbol for the animal portion of creation, and in the geometric pattern of the branches, divine order and design.

Nod *(page 17)* – Like Cain in the land of Nod, we sometimes lose our sense of direction. We wander through places with no signs, no paths or roads, no obvious way out.

Ararat *(page 18)* – In the desert we feel a distinct freshness in the air after a heavy rain. Beyond this clearing thunderstorm, the cloud-shrouded mountain suggests the new start that was Ararat.

*Babel *(page 21)* – This well-worn bulletin board speaks not only of the confusion of Babel but also of the power—and temporality—of language.

Ur *(page 22)* – We set off for the unknown, leaving behind the fortifications and foundations of human making.

*Asterisks mark Sundays for those who choose to begin this journey on Ash Wednesday and follow it through Lent

Notes on the Photographs

Shechem *(page 25)* – This gnarly old oak—wizened, weather-scarred, but still strong and imposing—reminds us of Abraham himself (whom we rarely think of as young!).

Mamre *(page 26)* – What we like about Sarah is that despite all that she has seen she retains a sense of wonder. We observe in her the care a mother shows toward her child.

Moriah *(page 29)* – Our view of this familiar story is turned upside down when we look up at the tree from anxious young Isaac's perspective.

Bethel *(page 30)* – As it was for Jacob, our journey of faith is a constant climb from darkness toward light.

Peniel *(page 33)* – We are unnerved by the thought of wrestling a shadowy, mysterious figure through the night—but fascinated by the blessing that came after the dawn.

*Goshen *(page 34)* – As strangers in Egypt, we are relieved to find life-giving water in such a dry land.

The Nile *(page 37)* – When we are overwhelmed by the world around us, we feel as vulnerable as the baby Moses, peering over the edge of his little basket bobbing in the reeds of the mighty Nile.

Horeb *(page 38)* – Although on our journey we don't expect to find burning bushes, we still encounter God in unexpected places.

The Red Sea *(page 41)* – The prospect of the towering wall of water crashing down upon us makes us tremble.

The Sinai Desert *(page 42)* – The day-in, day-out search for fresh water in the parched Sinai desert demanded constant attention from the Israelites. It is not difficult to imagine the disappointment of following dry stream traces for miles only to find that this lowest area has finally dried up as well.

Nebo *(page 45)* – With Moses we gaze into the morning mist and see the distant hills of the promised land.

Persia *(page 46)* – We too often dismiss rulers and leaders as secular and godless, associating them with the towers and fortresses they build and not with the purposes of God they might serve.

*Babylon *(page 49)* – We follow paths not always knowing where they'll lead us, but we journey onward.

Chebar *(page 50)* – The misty atmosphere over a meandering river suggests the mystery of things we cannot see.

Sheol *(page 53)* – Thoughts of the underworld make us shudder; we fear the jaws of damnation.

Tekoa *(page 54)* – Daily leading his sheep up the same trails, a solitary shepherd reminds us that the call of God can come to the most unexpected people in the least remarkable places.

Nineveh *(page 57)* – From a distant hill we see a vast city, looking at night like a galaxy of stars swirling in dark space.

Bethlehem *(page 58)* – During our journey we can easily overlook a small village nestled in a hillside.

Notes on the Photographs

Thebes *(page 61)* – Our pilgrimage is not always easy; sometimes destruction threatens us.

*Mount Paran *(page 62)* – Although we think of deserts as hot places, they can be even harsher at night when the wind picks up and temperatures plummet to near freezing. (The tracks of stars in the sky above St. Catherine's Monastery were caused by rotation of the earth during the six-minute exposure.)

Gaza *(page 65)* – Some historians say that Gaza has been captured and rebuilt more than any other city in the world. Gaza City's deserted beach stands as a stark reminder of the desolation of this place.

Bethel *(page 66)* – As we smile at the exuberance of this carefree boy in a park where Arab and Jewish children play together, we look for hope in our own cities.

Judah *(page 69)* – In many churches worshipers give offerings of fire in the form of small candles. The flickering flames seem reminiscent of faces: some brighter, some dimmer, some older, some newer.

Nazareth *(page 70)* – As the heavens open up over an abandoned farm near Nazareth, the dramatic sky recalls the contrast between the ordinariness of Mary and the spectacular message of the annunciation.

Cana *(page 73)* – On our journey through life we usually focus on the immediate world in front of us rather than scanning distant landscapes; the details are often more memorable than the panoramic vistas we have seen.

Capernaum *(page 74)* – When we visit this ancient synagogue in Capernaum, we realize that ruins can be more than historical remains if they help our faith come to life.

*The Sea of Galilee *(front cover and page 77)* – Quiet waters at the end of the day reflect the peacefulness of Galilee.

Sychar *(page 78)* – The universal connection between water and life gains a new dimension when Jesus offers the woman at the well living water for spiritual life.

Caesarea Philippi *(page 81)* – In the town that was Caesarea Philippi, this steeple holds steady as storm clouds swirl around —evoking the image of the Messiah who stands alone at the center.

Mount Tabor *(page 82)* – A beam of light illumines the place at the top of Mount Tabor where the transfiguration is said to have occurred.

Samaria *(page 85)* – When we encounter the barbed wire in the chancel window of this sealed-off church, we feel the frustration of wanting to go places we cannot. (A cross is formed by the mortar joints around the window.)

Jericho *(page 86)* – While the rest of the world rushed by, the man's blindness forced him to remain in the same place every day—until Jesus stopped to free him.

The Bethany Tomb *(page 89)* – On our journey we encounter both darkness and light, death and life.

*Bethphage *(page 90)* – The palm fronds radiate like rays of the sun; the hosannas of the morning echo through the ages.

Notes on the Photographs

Jerusalem *(page 93)* – We entrust ourselves to God's care, knowing that God alone can get us through life's foreboding passages.

The Mount of Olives *(page 94)* – This tortured, gnarly olive trunk evokes the conflicting moods of Holy Week.

Bethany *(page 97)* – As we journey through the countryside, we remember that there are also private places along the way.

Gethsemane *(page 98)* – As dusk approaches, we walk together up the hill outside the walls of Jerusalem. We enter this quiet garden and recall our places of prayer.

Golgotha *(page 101)* – This is not a place where we would linger—except for our grim fascination with rubble that looks like skulls and a cliff face that seems to drop all the way down to hell.

A Tomb in Jerusalem *(page 102)* – We sometimes question whether we can associate ordinary sites with significant spiritual events . . . But then we remember that Jesus was born in a barn, heralded by shepherds, raised by a carpenter, and executed like a common criminal: the ordinary made holy is the point.

*Galilee *(page 105)* – A new dawn.

Acknowledgments

The photographer would like to thank first and foremost Claudine Wagenaar, without whose extraordinary assistance before, during (from across the Atlantic), and after his trips to the Mideast this project would have been impossible to complete. Thanks also to Emma, Alexis, Bob, and the rest of the wonderful staff at St. Andrew's Hospice in Jerusalem, who provided a charming Scottish home away from home. Both author and photographer owe a debt of gratitude to Rachel and Yaakov Ariel, dear friends and generous hosts in Israel, and to Harriet Marty, wife and stepmother, for her assistance on the home front. Finally, Ann Rehfeldt at Augsburg Fortress went far beyond the call of duty, taking a personal interest in this endeavor and carefully shepherding it through the hills and valleys of the rocky publishing landscape. Her thoughtful editorial contributions have in countless ways enhanced both the pictures and the words herein. We sensed that through all the processes she and we were mutually undertaking the spiritual journey we have shared with the reader.